KAPUTNIKS

Peter Jay Shippy

Distributed by Independent Publishers Group
Chicago

Saturnalia Books
105 Woodside Rd.
Ardmore, PA 19003
info@saturnaliabooks.com

ISBN: 978-1-947817-28-9 (print) 978-1-947817-29-6 (eBook)
Library of Congress Control Number: 2020949459

Cover art and book design by Robin Vuchnich

Distributed by:
Independent Publishing Group
814 N. Franklin St.
Chicago, IL 60610
800-888-4741

Thanks to the editors of the following journals: *The American Poetry Review*, *The Antioch Review*, *Black-box Manifold*, *Caffeine Destiny*, *The Canary*, *The Common*, *Conduit*, *The Fairy Tale Review*, *Folio*, *Free Verse*, *Harvard Review*, *Incessant Pipe*, *Lady Churchill's Rosebud Wristlet*, *The Literary Review*, *Matrix*, *The Missouri Review*, *Okey-Panky*, *The Paris-American*, and *Sentence*.

for Charlotte

Contents

The Loury Glamours

A red vase set loose two white tulips.

Sour cherries and a drift of asparagus glistened a porcelain sink.

Lambs emerged from people in ways particular to the person.

A life like any other life.

A trussing needle and cotton thread, a pair of ruby Docs

add x-rays

subtract phalanges and gizzards but

we let the goldfish die, so the war began. We were ushered into the film palace. We lived on stale milk duds and the same film: *she was killed by a shotgun blast to the face.* One of us who wanted to be an equestrian rode a mop up and down the aisles. *Through the interrogation of her friends, and the reading of her letters and diaries, the detective became possessed.* One of us who wanted to be a vet combed our hair and pinched our arms. *He becomes suspicious of a clock with a secret lock.* One of us who wanted to be taller hung from balcony until he couldn't and fell into a mound of popcorn. *He falls asleep under her portrait only to be awakened by her—breaking into her own apartment.*

One of us who wants to be a dancer dances.

Toward the end of the war a tree branch started growing through one of the walls. Wild oats sprouted through the red carpet. An eclipse of moths covered the screen. *Goodbye, Mary. Goodbye, my love,* I whispered as we followed flashlights through corridors and the exit door to escape the top hat, into the night. One of us looked at the full moon and began to sing:

The needle-nose pliers have pin-bones for teeth.

A pan of boiling olive oil provides the best reflection.
Garlic bulbs keep the stew free of demons.

Dye your hair with the skin and skip town.

Make a boat, a rose, an onion from newspaper or find a child and write on its palm:

what makes the lamb love Mary so.

Curve Seen from the Parkway, Model City, 1966

A garden Buddha flashes into Buddha and back again.

Nouvelle Vague

It was time to shoot
the claw-footed tub scene—

bubbles, soap, and rubber
rats scratching lines on

porcelain. You enlisted
a goosenecked brush to play

the pensive sea serpent.
I set the orchestra

to ballad to give our wreck
that deep-sixed look.

Steam veiled the mold stars—
our iguana asterism—

no use trying to steer.
We were irretrievable.

I finger-framed your mouth:
I can hear something

breathing where I breathe.
Will you take my picture?

Agriculture

To soften their mouths
they practice kissing

the earth. His face pales
like virus, a page

of deleting words.
Her eyes are seeds, wild-

flowers, perfect for
his little catapult.

The Little Capital of the Past

You made a set of rooms
from papier-mâché

and plunked them
onto the rooftop

of a terrace house
in the Blue-veined District—

we lived like squabs.
No one the wiser.

We warmed our home
with a ruptured Farfisa.

The icebox suffered bouts
of lightheaded opera.

I earned a little more
taking-in wet Polaroids

to dry on the line with
knobby tops and peppers.

When the static ebbed
we quit our own sweet time

and chanced out, tracing
the half-world, passing

wig shops, tobacconists,
oyster carts, turning left

at the Punjab Spa right
into The Silhouette

to quicken against others
on the sawdust floor.

Our hands grew into
silver Ray-guns—zap—

we lived like squabs.
No one the wiser.

We warmed our home
with a ruptured Farfisa.

A Game of Elimination

The music stops and one is left standing.

They're told to leave the house and wait outside, with us.

We press our faces against the window and report on dessert: honey cake. And mint ice cream? Pistachio?

We wonder about the chairs: Shaker, we agree.

We consider the music: Was it really fair for the birthday boy to play his own song—on a Theremin! —as we played along?

One of us turns from the party and stares past the swing-set and fire-pit, into the wild orchard. We hear beetles boring, turning applewood into a desert. One of us walks

> we walk into town
> to catch the bus.

> It's snowing, night.
> The girl next

> to us smells
> like lambing.

> She's wearing
> her father's

leather vest hung
with patches—

Motorpsycho,
Sinner. She listens

to beats so stung
our seat vibrates

yes, yes, maybe
as we watch

the birthday boy
rip open our gifts

and toss train sets,
tablets, gift cards

into the corner.
He pins our ribbons

to his long nips.
One of us cuts

his cake as one
steps off a bus

letting the snow
dumb our tongues.

Uncomposed

At dusk, a spill
of blue iris
grows nervous.

An Afterlife

The mummy unwound her bandages, inserted her organs, false eyes,
   and went out for a bite.

They make a lovely spinach gnocchi at Jimmy's, she thought, and
   headed toward the river.

The sky was porcine, fat and pink.

She wore a cardigan, rope sandals, and itchy blue socks

She passed Monsieur Phot's Pho, smelled lemongrass, heard moon
   lutes, and almost walked in, but no, Jimmy's, the lovely spinach,
   the gnocchi.

She stopped to listen to a Cyclops play a tango on a cello.

Her face was reflected in his wrap-around shade.

She wished she had brought a sharp pair of scissors to trim her
   sutures.

I'm not getting any older, she thought, and tossed a dollar into his
   cowboy hat.

All cities are translations of other cities.

Here, she was still tongue-tied so she hid in the gaps between source
and commentary. Community?

She liked cowls with ears, magazine subscriptions, and mongrel
salukis.

She preserved her essences in a Russian doll, not canopic jars.

The park was filled with touch football and picnics.

A pigeon was remembering the tall cliffs of east Africa.

The mummy took a soft left at the monument to the veterans of the
Uncelebrated Wars.

At Jimmy's, she sat in the courtyard and sipped a glass of house red.

A couple asked her to take their picture.

Conjoined twins played Debussy.

When the waiter brought Ossobuco she didn't complain.

She didn't say a thing.

Asterisk

My parents used to
but now they don't
because of their death
they've become cranky
unwilling to help me
work or eat or address
the stars on the ceiling
twitching like mussels
because of their grit
under my tongue.

October, First Snow

I walk backwards
in your footsteps.

A red sheet twists
on the clothesline.

Winter branches
bend toward our house

hoping to sip
from our bowl of suns.

Sparrows flood
the window, darkening

the bed where my head
learns to speak

by rolling across
your skin, unlike us

a bird reveals its soul
in the flock.

Colonial Memory

When I was a boy the best piano diviners were elephants. African elephants, mostly, because of their longer ears. In preparation for my 5th grade recital my mother hired Dr. Glass and his assistant, Hannibal.

It was fascinating to watch their lissome noses poke around our bungalow. They found a snooker ball that had rolled under the idiot box. They found a rook in a rook's nest. Who knew my grandmother's hairpins were propping open the dormer window? They found my great-uncle's narwhal tusk dentures in my great-uncle's mouth, but they never did find our Schimmel.

After their search we recused ourselves to the patio for cloudy lemonade, and Dr. Glass hosed me off.

There's a fair amount of serious writing

about people who believe
that a dead person—maybe
their brother, is watching them
from above or below or
from their bedroom closet,
animating an oxford shirt,
ash blue, with a penguin logo,
extending the left sleeve
sideways and bending
90-degrees at the elbow
downward: stop.

Now there is one more.

Hatchings

Parades always made her tired, so it wasn't surprising that the assassin fell asleep on the roof.

As she napped, the roof became quite crowded.

A family of six had a picnic, fried chicken and potato salad. Their baby gummed lime gelato.

The super pretended to repair the cooling duct. His toolbox was full of ale.

An octogenarian who had learned to swim in the Baltic Sea leaped into the wooden water tower for her daily laps.

A boy wearing an aviator's hat fed his pigeons. One of the birds, Charles, was worried about Amelia, his mate. She hadn't returned from their afternoon flight. The boy understood, so he stroked Charles' head and whistled, "Volière."

The octogenarian climbed out of the tower only to discover that she had forgotten her towel. The family cleared their picnic and after apologizing for the crumbs and green stains, wrapped her in their plaid blanket. She invited the family, the boy, and Charles to her apartment for chocolate covered prunes.

The Super emptied his last bottle, closed his toolbox, walked toward the railing to take in the view and almost stepped on the assassin. He noticed her rifle. Italian. A Marinetti. He picked it up and looked through the scope. There was an old hen circling the building. The sky was melting like a Creamsicle. He clicked off the gun's safety and tucked it under the assassin's arm.

The assassin dreamed that she was a girl in her bedroom having a pillow fight with her sister.

Feathers fell through the air, ticking their cheeks.

Forensic

By each crime
I commit
myself to you.

Status Report

After years of digging my tunnel
I reach my neighbor's foundation.

From picks and shovels to laser drills.
Progress is a beautiful thing. Alas,

the object of my excavation moved
not long after I began burrowing.

I don't feel the same about my new neighbor.
Not yet. Should I collapse my tunnel?

Should I flood it and stock it with blind,
pale fish? Times being what they are

I'll stand pat. I'll ravel my sins.
It's a beautiful thing, my tunnel.

A Fatal Language

for Attila Jozef

One day we spoke Hungarian.

Which day?
I wouldn't dare say, see

since we all spoke Hungarian
we understood each other
and didn't know that we were
speaking Hungarian, quite
odd, we thought, of the barks
in our throats. Croup? Loupe?

It wasn't until we shipped
from New Bedford to Paprika
with a load of codswallop
that we understood: ah,
we're speaking Hungarian.

According to our smart phone
it's the knottiest language
in the world to learn. Now
we're too frightened to say boo.

Nightwork

Have you heard?

The one-man band disbanded.

His widow keeps his knee cymbals in the garden, to collect rainwater
for hummingbirds.

His foot-cello's toe-bow props open the garage door, so, now, feral cats have
a place to shelter.

Remember his baby Steinway? The one he played with his eyelashes? The
keys were donated to that woman who makes dentures for babies.

His ashes were poured into shotgun shells. His wife used the suicide
Winchester on his marker... an applique of sorts, I guess.

Once, I think I saw a baker using his squeezebox to cool her macaroons.

His wife trained the moonflowers growing outside their bedroom window
to climb his bassoonette.

That's how I saw her.

I was snipping the flowers, to steal the instrument, when I peaked in the
window. She was standing on a stool, changing a light bulb.

Later, she folded clothes and ironed some shirts. She put on a record and jumped up and down to turbo-charged guitars.

She undressed and planted a Day-Glo transistor radio—his? —under her pillow.

We fell asleep listening to late innings from the coast.

With the Leaves

After last call
our postmaster
delivers the barber
to his shop
and sets off
toward the lake
balancing
on a ball bat
moonlight
casting off
her shorn skull
one more
surrender
to make.

"The Metamorphosis"

When time travel became possible, those machines could only go back-
wards. So, we cleared our prisons. Sent those no-goodniks back to the Neo-
lithic where they developed farming which led to the domestication of cattle
and pigs, the invention of the wheel, mathematics, and pottery which led to
smelting, writing, and cities, Persepolis, which led to casting, forging and
steel, the Hebrew bible and the Vedas, which led to the Sphinx and Greece
and Rome, the Tang, the Inca, and Aztec, which led to revolutions, Galileo
and Newton, American and French, which led to punk rock, Boston, The
Rathskeller, 1979, where my grandmother slammed into my grandfather
at a Black Flag show, which led to me, under my covers, shivering, fifteen,
reading this story about a bug that is somehow written about me.

Hunger

The barometer, its hurricane.

The Eels of Desire

for Adam Hammer

Eugene took a break
from making

funerary boats
from kite string

and Popsicle sticks
to have a snack—

unagi, Moxie—
in the deep end

of his kidney-
shaped pool.

He couldn't fix
the last time

there was water.
Or swimmers.

The bugs sure get
sorry at night

he thought, so blue
they turn to metal—

often from Finland.
Eugene watched

a starling perch
on the diving board.

He looked into
her umlaut eyes

and tossed a roll
her way.

After eating
she pecked the drain

for algae, and sang
that Weimar

standard, "You
and My Mischiefs":

Close your eyes
they won't see you

Plug your ears
they won't hear you

Pinch your nose
they won't smell you

Cover your mouth
and...."

He climbed out
of the pool

and used his
chopsticks

to divine
the weather:

*clammy, close,
scare quotes*

*moving-in
from the coast.*

Gyro Hero, at 4:00 AM

A fly on the fritz
rubs its tits

against the screen.
I open the door

to evict our king
from holy Thebes.

My lamb bleats.
The light bulb fizzes.

Exeunt. me.

Saint Gravity

After my parents kicked
a chairlift lifted me
into the attic
to tend their flock
of christening gowns.
This is the way
our people mourn.
At dawn I'd prop
a dormer and release
newspaper kites
to inform the neighbors
of a moon landing…
sales on sheer hose…
my monster breathes.

Most days I laid
on dunes of dried milk
calling-up Janus words
from mother's list—
bound, cleave, fast, dust.
When leaves fell
from our blue cedar
egg-light glossed
the floorboards
and I scrabbled to
the stellar plash

and lapped until
I mustered out
an odd soul.

At last I was small
enough to fit
into a rosette frock

and take my place
on the Avenue of...
next to you.

The Girl in the Blue Öyster Cult Onesie

My job?

To defend our fair city from haywire robots, he said, as he eradicated the crust from his daughter's croque-monsieur.

She nodded, but her face was under the moon.

I'll write my essay on Mom, she sighed, heavy, heavy as the anvil-sized backpack she dragged from the kitchenette.

He looked at his other one, the girl in the Blue Öyster Cult onesie. She was noshing on Godzilla's patchwork tail.

She growled. He bellowed.

That one, he thought, understands me.

She & I?

  Simpatico.

The Farmer's Market

We look up
at a flock
of duck bellies
fall already
says the man
with bouquets
of speckled trout
spread across
his card table
as a kid with
livid hair plays
"Cruel Rhubarb"
on bass sax
while the man
employs a set
of needle nose
pliers to cull
fish teeth which
he drops into
a matchbox.
I drop a bill
into the kid's
colossal case
and wonder
how does she

get home how
do I get home
before dinner
gums its way through
butcher paper?

An Old Pond

After he croaked, I broke him down and soaked his sweetbreads in a
barrel of sake for a week.

Then I dusted the poet in sea salt ginger, and yuzu zest.

I lit the charcoal and like a cicada through a rock, I slid a skewer
through his thymus.

Splash.

Halloween Party

Like cormorants
children bob
for eels.

Glam

We gathered the broken-limbed kids and hauled them to the river.

Sink or swim, we taunted, which was fucked.

The river was 10-yards wide and a foot deep.

Simply, we were awfully keen for their white casts, their plasters' blaze
of Hancocks and erotic pictographs.

And we envied their allowances.

One was allowed to wear her Indian headdress to church service.

One gnawed Ticonderoga's until his teeth were grey.

And we were left, with their chores.

We trashed the Chinese take-out.

We walked the cat, washed the grass, and mowed the dishes.

We were made to wheel one of them to the beach and push her through
wet sand so she could catch a tan.

We stole their stepmothers' blush bikini bottoms from the clothesline,
and took the blame.

It was the summer our parents Kamalized their sutras, becoming
     cuckoos, pigeons, red vipers, parrots, bees, dragons, mongooses,
     tigers, blue-headed teals, tigers, and Himalayan quail.

It was the summer Ziggy Stardust died.

Tinder, kindling, fuel.

So, we built a fire.

We ploughed the fields and scattered ashes and Morton's salt to
     redouble our hate.

One sang Cat Stevens, *baby I love you, baby I love you,* as we tossed his
     crutches into the bonfire.

One quoted Samuel, *we are like water spilled on the ground, which
     cannot be gathered up again.*

We used oyster hammers to crack their plaster shells, revealing their
     soft, pink vibrations.

We masked their faces with scarlet hose
                              heave-ho
                              we let go.

Ain't that close to love?

When we got home our father was father again, rubbing train oil into
        my new mitt, stuffing a ball into the webbing and tying it off like
        a roast, with butcher's string, breaking it in, breaking us in.

We were awful frightened of his smell, a loco inside a bull, and that look
        in his tired eyes.

Our mothers were talking with their mothers, shaking with curses, so
        out came the clippers.

Our fathers shaved our heads and made us pack our bloody hair into
        envelopes and hand them over to those drags in the hospital.

Our locks were burned with myrrh in silver censers as we chanted
        die already,
            under our breaths.

You see, we did not repent

because we were jealous of their days at home, watching old men solve
        homicides, eating cheeseburgers, and sweet potato fries and

we envied their visits from the prayer squad

and the clumsy hand-jobs

and the healing
       their second chance, we hated
            those broke, growing whole.

Expulsion

After he was sent home
his mother prepared
his favorite meal:

nighttime.

The Lost Colony

Near dawn I deliver
baskets of buttered toast
and pencil sharpeners
to each cabin. Often
I'm summoned to serve
as a model or provide
rhymes or extra digits
for counting measures.
An Olivetti's clack-clack
causes worms to rise
and enter a novella.
On my smoking break
I shuck little necks—
the painter needs trays.
Each visitant employs
unique techniques—claps,
footsie, carrier rat,
or blank stares—to transmit
their luncheon orders.
Most choose fluffernutter.
When the sea winds attack
her blackboard, the composer
must take her music inside.
On my smoking break
I touch up the haint paint

on their porch ceilings.
Din-din is always potluck
so, each evening they
starve to death then play
their only game: One Question:
Are their thimbles for toes?
Some say they can't say. You?
Is cereal gazpacho?
On my smoking break
I smoke until I'm blue
in the face. At last I bear
the lightbulb from cabin
to cabin so they can see
their hands as they pray.

Sheepy

In a meadow he asked
an entomologist

about an insect
trekking across his

bare chest. She used
her tongue to escort

that iridescent pinch
to his tongue, then said,

The whole enchilada
is beetle. Cin cin.

Kaputnik

She was sitting on my bed grinding birds into powder.

Was that a reed sparrow, or a long player?

Mother believed that waking to birdsong was a healthy way to begin the day. And toast. Honey. Milk. Sometimes strawberry milk. And almond butter. I heard her knife serrating brown bread.

Not a house knife? Not a sparrow.

She was sitting on my bed grinding red birds into powder.

Red birds?

Cardinals. Robins' breasts. Tanagers. Certain parrots. Certain parrots from South America from documentary films. And songs. Cartoons. A woodpecker? Argentina. Brazil. Or Belize. But that's central America, yes?

Or pets.

Pets escape their owners. Owners abandon their pets. Signs stapled to telephone poles and trees. Phone numbers. Rewards. Cash. Gift certificates. Free tattoos.

No. Not pets. Not birds.

Pills. Red pills.

She was sitting on my bed with a pestle and a cutting board grinding pills into powder.

"One more potion," she said.

She opened a packet and used her pinky to mix Sweet 'n Low into the pounce.

"Smile," mother said, licking her finger, "we're almost better."

Fear of Flying

caterpillar
awoke to find
itself still
caterpillar
returning
to its book
to find
a solution
to its phobia
before eating
all the words.

Hi Dalai

Picture me outside Dunkin' in the parking lot chucking glazed Munchkins at pigeons, when his motorcade sweeps in.

There are Hummers, a Lama-mobile with a bulletproof viewing bubble, and a saffron-robed security unit, that spreads-out, spinning digital prayer wheels on their cell phones, searching for Maoists or Warniks, with a grudge.

I dig the way their earpieces wiggle, like brain-slurping beetles.

All at once his pop-o-matic dome cracks open, and the Holy Man Himself steps out to buy hot tea, a French Cruller, and invoke the Great Compassion of the Buddha.

The patrons form a greeting line. The Lama issues blessings and removes his bare hands from his faux-fur muff to press flesh and smile.

He smiles at me and brushes his Lama thumb across my lip. Powdered sugar, the Lama thinks, and he licks his Lama thumb and everyone laughs as his Lama pupils dilate.

Now we are stoned. The Lama and I are stoned in the parking lot in moonlight.

Each goes his own way.

Singing Beach

After I left home, I worked in a store on the coast that sold little hurricanes. They were kept in cobalt canning jars with lightning lids. When the humidity rose, the wooden shelves creaked.

People used them to water their tomatoes or to ruin a rival's garden party. For a few weeks, it was a rage for teenagers to hide them in unlucky cars.

But after a girl swallowed her tempest the store had to be closed. They never found her body.

The owner gave me a jar in lieu of a last check.

I keep it in my basement, wrapped in damp, thick canvas. I imagine her when it begins to chirr.

I'll never sell it.

Giacometti

I live with
a number

of his sculptures
in my studio

apartment.
I don't know why

they appear.
Just last night

while watching
Helsinki

CCTV
on my wristwatch

I thought I heard
hummingbirds

sipping from
my toilet. Yet

I found *Woman*
with Her Throat Cut

in the tub.
Who wants *that*

under the suds?
Not a day passes

I don't come home
to a figure, gnawed

and bent toward
walking from one wall

to its opposite.
Some are shorter

than my thumb.
From my belly I

envy how moonlight
graces their skin.

Once, I opened
my toaster oven

and found not
pizza dogs but

The Palace
at 4 AM.

That was nice
at 3 AM.

An Eel Soup Digression

Because the navigator didn't understand that the crease in the map depicted a crease in the sea, the ship had to weigh anchor. The captain forced the navigator to row a dinghy through the line, to reckon its effects.

Meanwhile, in the galley, the cook was creating a bouillabaisse—conger eel, sea robins, fennel, cod bones, bouquet garni, saffron, mussels, olive oil, garlic, white wine, smoke of the afterlife, French bread, cayenne pepper, little neck clams, tomato paste, and Thibault, the very lobster that was conducted through the streets of Paris by Gérard de Nerval.

Concurrently, the navigator was remembering a poem about a boy who thought the crescent moon was a broken moon and the stars were its pieces. He could smell the soup. At least, he thought, as the water began to churn, I'll have something good to eat tonight.

Go-kart Mozarts

As kids we dragged classic furniture. I had a souped-up Aeron side chair.
My buddy was a demon with Chicago cocktail tables. The woman who
collected pop bottles for Christ cast kittens when the Christmas tree was lit
and we got loose on Lockport hurtling toward the sand traps by the canal.

Once, after a skirmish or three we were smoking on a stoop when a man on
a Van Der Rohe daybed challenged us to sprint for pink slips. Before we
could answer a palooka in an ebony Noguchi hit a fire hydrant and burst
into sawdust.

And that was that.

The antique dealers came down hard and street racing was banned.

Yet, even today, decades later, the smell of burning angels and pine brings
conjunctivitis to my eyes.

Two Gospels

1

My ribs are sardines.

They beg me to turn the key.

But when I do, I arrest. Or is that dancing?

The fish are not pleased.

It reminds them of their death, below decks, above the sea, covered in salt, rocking, singing their sardine songs as the fishermen cleaned their blades with red ale.

I grab the freezer door to steady myself and it opens. I stick my head inside. What a world! Swedish meatballs, peas, vodka, pearl onions, samosas, ice cream and a cow's heart.

The light bulb is a white dwarf, humming, radiating, dreaming of its future as a black dwarf.

My chest ripples. The fins sense water. They want to dive into the vanilla lava, swim to the ocean in the center of the earth and transform into a shrewdness of evian Eves.

2

Later, outside, I sit on my stoop, with my friends, Nyquil & Bubble Yum.

A clutter of uniformed school children pass by.

Each one of those angels will tease the skinned rabbits in the butcher shop
window, I know.

I scratch my neck and there it is, the key. Caught in my throat.
I finish the bottle and whisper to my bonefish: *Vivat*—

> *don't swoon*
> *I'm greasing*
>
> *the track, soon*
> *we'll all be free.*

Sex in the Quaker Graveyard in Woonsocket

The morning after
one could read Christian
off the other one's skin.

Shrinkwraps

The Ship Trapped in Ice

The pilot's cheeks are cloudberries.

The crow's nest is stuffed with rum nips.

The first mate and the third mate are making a fourth mate
in the powder room

       boom

      spar, anchor, keel, mizzen.

The captain's tied to the mast; her ears are stuffed with wax lips.

     Sirens or clowns?

The figurehead frowns, ashamed to front a ship of philosophers.

I set my kettle to boil.

I pop their cube into my cup.

I can't wait for their plot to quicken.

Overtime

On his desk he kept a working station.

One evening, a bus stopped. The door opened and two passengers disembarked.

They looked confused, lost. Before they could reboard, the bus peeled away, leaving skid marks on his leather blotter.

Silly driver, he thought. The sign taped to his thumbtack jar was clear as crystal: Train Station.

One traveler leaned against his stapler and smoked a stinker. The other sat on a pillow of pencil shavings.

Well.

He crumbled aspirin and snowed it over their heads and onto their tongues. When they nodded off, he used a marker to apply black Xs to their eyes. He crossed their arms on their chest.

Bon nuit, he whispered. *Don't worry, in the main The Downeaster is quite punctual.*

He opened a drawer and pulled out a paper cup connected to a string. *Hey there, you'll need to add a coffin car to the 10:15.*

He put their luggage with the rest, in an old clay ashtray that he had made for his father.

Finally, he used liquid paper to outline their shapes.

We, said the Wren

I didn't know vampires taste like Gatorade. Nor did I know hairs made fair with weeds, milk thistle, and lambs quarters.

Where our mouths came together, blue roots.

I was marooned in bird pathology: raptors and sick jazz until I swapped my name for your face.

We bit eyeholes into wool caps, traveled over a bridge of braids hung over a river, yellow reeds, my window, smeared with sap from the old plane tree.

Sow. Deadhead. Knead.

Spring Cleaning

I wipe your eyeball prints from my window.

You won't see me again.

Attar

As I wait for my cake to cool, I realize it's been forever since I'd harvested the nectar from a Japanese honeysuckle.

Calyx, my sister, lived in our old house at the edge of the forest ripping the reproductive organs off those yellow flowers.

She sold them to concerns in XYZ.

Don't fret. Those sweet things are to blame for displacing hundreds of native species. They deserved the pinch.

Then she met a huntsman, took up meat, and moved to Alaska.

I suppose that Calyx is dead, but the fine points of her demise are beyond my reach.

Pickaxe? Orgasm? Icicle? Orgasm?

When the tin rhino on my counter brings his brass cymbals together—crash—I may eat. It's a white cake with white frosting dusted with habanero.

> *Happy birthday to me,*
> *I live in a zoo,*
>
> *I look like a monkey*
> *And I smell like one, too.*

Kindergarten Tour, the Curley School, Boston

They sang the phonebook
those ruffed figures

wearing respirators
near the yellow wall

aiming blow torches
at barrels of myrrh,

the docent said, *I mean*
I think it's a scream

that we're alive.
Today! Don't you?

What Leaf? What Mushroom?

If you see leaves
that seem

to be walking
get down

on your knees
and look.

You may find
an ant

a leafcutter
is taking it away.

If not, stay down, you may be ceremonious. You may be consumed. A blue
fungus? A white flower? Jagged leaves? Pill bugs? Armies and fleets of her
majesty's cells? Frith dust? Hosts? Death-caps? The choir's ear? A factory
strange to the tongue? False slippers? Midges? Pears and weather?

Relax. Enjoy the sun. Sip honeysuckle. Listen to birdsong.

Soon, the ants
will come

to stroke you
with their antennae

and carry you
below the pain

a cool chamber
your new home.

After Humankind

towers of giraffe sport harmonica neck racks.

Lieder

One morning, a man and his daughter are eating cold pizza with black olives and linguica as they watch, *Yo Gabba Gabba.* The character named Gooble looks like a ghost with sad, red, clown lips. He's crying (he always cries) because he doesn't want to halfsie his red paint. So, the inhabitants of GabbaLand sing a song about sharing art supplies.

The man wonders if his daughter knows that Gooble is an actor wearing a costume. She's 5. She'll start kindergarten in a month. Will her classmates know that Gooble is an actor dressed like a ghost with sad, red, clown lips? Will they share art supplies?

Will they understand that his daughter has refined the collision of genius *and* beauty!?

He offers her the last slice. She uses her purple chimpsticks to pluck an olive and stick it up his nose as Muno, Foofa, and DJ Lance Rock rap:

> *Don't cry, don't weep*
> *Hokusai, Hans Arp*

> *Don't bay, don't woe*
> *Man Ray, Frieda Kahlo*

> *Don't bray, don't whinge*
> *Paul Klee, Maya Lin*

Don't boo, don't hiss
Jeff Koons, Eva Hesse

The man takes his daughter's hand and together they crazy dance to a toy piano's delirious longing.

Rabbit

The moon is full.
The fox is full.

My burrow is half-full.

The Girl Who Trod

Once a girl put my head in her backpack and took it for a walk. She added in a few russets, too, so I wouldn't feel lonely. I couldn't see a thing, but I didn't complain. It was fine to be away from my heartbeats.

I heard church bells and car horns. I smelled chocolate and my favorite perfume, Pretty Peach. I tasted earth.

When we stopped walking, she took me out and set me on a redwood picnic bench. Behind me, I heard the sea. She stuffed my mouth with wet sand and began to show me her backpack's clip-ons: a dayglo crow, a speckled egg, a scarab, and a flying saucer.

I wondered what my legs were up to.

Were my fingers thrumming the air, playing air piano?

Why did the singer sound like a seagull? Was her voice broken?

Before she left, the girl turned me around so I could look at the water and the white sun.

Am I hungry? Who will put my body to bed?

Antistrophe

Sometimes young people fill me with helium and let go.

In the air, I bring my knees together, rubbing notes to warn the birds that I'm riding their tack.

Sometimes I brush chimneys; sometimes I break satellite dishes.

When children see me, they throw rocks, hoping to help, hoping to instigate my descent.

Once, a man, standing on the edge of a roof waved. Did he believe that we were striped, of the same character? Maybe he leapt to join me. Maybe he was stuck in his gutter.

Sometimes my neck snares a telephone wire and I hear you, wishing me well.

When dogs see me they bark and snarl, hoping to guide me toward the catch of a radio tower.

Once, I saw a woman crying at a funeral, or was it a ceremony? Had she won the great prize? Had her father died? Either way, she wasn't prepared to deliver speech so the crowd lengthened, the chorus swayed like a field of goldenrod, to fill her absence.

Miles later I sailed over a mountain dog, harnessed to a sled, piled with corncockle, pillows, and a russeting girl who scowled as she figured what weather I resembled. Fog? Rain?

One dictionary definition of children is *inhabitants*, and I guess that's true, once they occupy your thoughts they never leave, even the ones who pray that you're a snow cloud.

Sometimes young people gas me enough that I make the impasto-capped steppes and slip like a wet noodle, through the mull, toward the sea.

I aim for a star but hope that I make it to one those islets in the bay, to rest, to stitch my wounds, and sketch a russeting girl running over a field of goldenrod, miles later.

North Station

A huddle of Assisi
in camo hoodies

pass smoke, exhaling
Corona coronas.

I wish I were a fox
sparrow. I'd drop

my disguise and flee
into their pockets

of cells and seeds
and fare-thee-well.

Shy

This film leaves me
in a close shot

dusk, snow
veils my eyes:

fried eggs under
onion skin.

Spring

Not a single UFO in the sky!
I remove my aluminum crown....